Slow-Cooker recipes

W9-CAU-307

Slow-Cooker Tips & Tricks

For easy clean-up, spray your slow cooker with non-stick vegetable spray before you begin.

For best results, fill your slow cooker 1/2 to 3/4 full. Food will be tastier and more tender.

No peeking! Unless the recipe calls for stirring, try not to lift the lid as your food cooks...it lets heat escape.

It's easy to put your slow-cooker meal together the night before. Just peel and chop up meats and vegetables, then refrigerate in separate plastic zipping bags. The next morning, toss everything into the slow cooker.

Ground meats should be browned and drained before using in a slow cooker recipe. Other meats don't need to be browned unless the recipe says to do so.

Some veggies like potatoes and carrots take longer to cook in a slow cooker. Chop them up fairly small or slice thinly.

Thaw or rinse frozen veggies before placing them in your slow cooker. Otherwise, they'll keep your dish from heating up as quickly as possible.

Slow cookers can sometimes dilute seasonings over a long cooking time...flavorful dried herbs and spices are best added near the end of cooking.

The first day of school or a Saturday filled with family events usually means a busy morning, so why not make Overnight Raisin-Nut Oatmeal the night before? Putting it together ahead of time means less fuss in the kitchen and a great start to the day!

Overnight Raisin-Nut Oatmeal   *Makes 4 servings*

1/4 c. brown sugar, packed
1 T. butter, melted
1/4 t. salt
1/2 t. cinnamon
1 c. quick-cooking oats,
   uncooked

1 c. apple, cored, peeled
   and minced
1/2 c. raisins
1/2 c. chopped nuts
2 c. milk

Place ingredients in a greased slow cooker; mix well. Cover and cook on low setting overnight, about 8 to 9 hours.

An easy way to core apples...slice fruit in half and then use
a melon baller to scoop out the core.

Harvest Apple Butter

Makes 4 jars

4 lbs. apples, cored and
    quartered
1 c. apple cider
2-1/2 c. sugar
1 t. cinnamon

1 t. ground cloves
1/2 t. allspice
4 1/2-pint canning jars
    and lids, sterilized

Place apples and cider in a slow cooker; cover and cook on high setting for 10 hours or overnight. Sift through a food mill; return pulp to slow cooker, discarding solids. Stir in remaining ingredients. Cook, uncovered, on high setting for one hour. Spoon into hot sterilized jars, leaving 1/4-inch headspace. Wipe rims; secure with lids and rings. Process in a boiling water bath for 10 to 15 minutes; set jars on a towel to cool. Check for seals.

A quick gift! Give a jar of homemade Sweet Apricot Preserves with a loaf of freshly baked bread wrapped in a pretty linen tea towel.

Sweet Apricot Preserves

Makes 4 jars

16-oz. pkg. dried apricots
1-3/4 c. sugar
3-1/2 c. water

4 1/2-pint canning jars
   and lids, sterilized

Finely chop apricots in a food processor; place in a slow cooker. Stir in sugar and water; cover and cook on high setting for 2-1/2 hours, stirring twice. Uncover and continue cooking on high setting until thickened, about 2 hours; stir occasionally. Spoon into hot sterilized jars, leaving 1/4-inch headspace. Wipe rims; secure with lids and rings. Process in a boiling water bath for 10 to 15 minutes; set jars on a towel to cool. Check for seals.

Fill a slow cooker with a welcoming hot beverage during
an open house...surround with crisp cookies and let
guests serve themselves!

Mom's Cranberry Tea

Makes 20 to 25 servings

3 cinnamon sticks
30 whole cloves
4 qts. water, divided
16-oz. can jellied cranberry
    sauce

2 6-oz. cans frozen orange
    juice concentrate, thawed
1 c. sugar
6 T. lemon juice

Combine cinnamon sticks, cloves and 2 cups water in a small saucepan; bring to a boil and boil for 10 minutes. In a large bowl, combine cranberry sauce, orange juice, sugar and lemon juice; add boiling liquid, straining cinnamon sticks and cloves. Pour mixture and remaining water into a slow cooker; cover and cook on low setting to keep warm while serving.

On a cool evening, invite friends over to enjoy a crackling fire,
warm English Cider and a favorite movie.

English Cider

Makes 6 to 8 servings

1/2 c. brown sugar, packed	2 cinnamon sticks
1-1/2 qts. apple cider	2 t. whole cloves
1 t. whole allspice	1 orange, sliced and seeded

Combine ingredients in a slow cooker. Spices can be placed in a tea strainer, if preferred, or added loose. Cover and cook on low setting for 2 to 8 hours. Strain before serving if necessary.

Let your slow cooker be your party helper, keeping meatballs or chicken wings warm and cheesy dips hot and bubbly!

Zesty Meatballs

Makes 30 servings

1 c. catsup
1 c. tomato sauce
1 c. grape juice

1 c. apple jelly
5 lbs. frozen meatballs

Combine all ingredients except meatballs in a slow cooker; mix well.
Cover and cook on low setting for one hour, stirring occasionally until
ingredients are well blended. Add meatballs; cover and cook on low
setting for 4 to 5 hours.

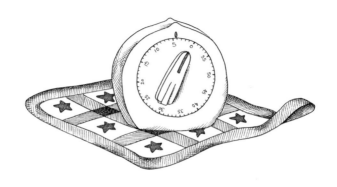

Want to change the cooking time of a slow cooker recipe?
It's simple...one hour of cooking on high equals 2 to
2-1/2 hours on low.

Teenie Party Weenies

2 16-oz. pkgs. cocktail weiners   12-oz. jar grape jelly
12-oz. bottle chili sauce

Combine all ingredients in a slow cooker. Cover and cook on low for
6 to 8 hours.

Make no-fuss hard-boiled eggs in your slow cooker! Cover
6 eggs with water in the slow cooker, cover and cook on
low for 3-1/2 hours. They'll be perfectly hard-boiled for
use in salads, sandwiches or even for Easter eggs.

Honey-Garlic Chicken Wings

Makes 8 to 12 servings

3 lbs. chicken wings
salt and pepper to taste
1 c. honey
1/2 c. soy sauce

2 T. catsup
2 T. oil
1 clove garlic, minced

Sprinkle chicken wings with salt and pepper; place in a slow cooker and set aside. In a mixing bowl, combine remaining ingredients and mix well. Pour sauce over wings. Cover and cook on low setting for 6 to 8 hours.

Send a big plastic zipping bag filled with Life-of-the-Party Snack Mix to your favorite college student...a welcome gift any time of year!

Life-of-the-Party Snack Mix   *Makes about 10 cups*

2 c. bite-size crispy wheat cereal
   squares
2 c. bite-size crispy corn cereal
   squares
2 c. bite-size crispy rice cereal
   squares
3 c. thin pretzel sticks

13-oz. jar mixed nuts
2 T. grated Parmesan cheese
1 t. garlic salt
1/2 t. seasoned salt
1/3 c. butter, melted
1/3 c. Worcestershire sauce

In a large bowl, mix together cereals, pretzels and nuts along with
Parmesan cheese, garlic salt and seasoned salt. Pour butter and
Worcestershire sauce over mixture; combine gently with hands. Pour
into a slow cooker; cover and cook on low setting for 3 to 4 hours.
Spread hot snack mix onto baking sheets lined with paper towels; let
dry for at least one hour, letting the towels absorb excess moisture.
Store in airtight containers.

Some like it hot...try using extra-spicy salsa and
Mexican-flavor pasteurized processed cheese spread
in your Fiesta Taco Dip for extra zing!

Fiesta Taco Dip

Makes about 3-1/2 cups

16-oz. pkg. pasteurized
    processed cheese spread,
    cubed
2 8-oz. pkgs. cream cheese,
    softened
16-oz. jar salsa

1-1/4 oz. pkg. taco seasoning
    mix
1 lb. ground beef, browned
    and drained
corn or tortilla chips

Combine all ingredients except chips in a slow cooker. Cover and cook
on low setting until cheeses melt, about one to 1-1/2 hours, stirring
frequently. Serve with corn or tortilla chips for dipping.

Give extra taste to recipes that use cream cheese by trying one that's flavored...chive, garlic, jalapeño or sun-dried tomato. Yummy!

Hot Crab Dip

Makes about 4 cups

3 8-oz. pkgs. cream cheese,
  cubed and softened
1/4 to 1/2 c. milk
2 6-1/2 oz. cans crabmeat,
  drained

1/2 c. green onion, chopped
1 t. prepared horseradish
1-1/2 t. Worcestershire sauce
assorted snack crackers

Combine all ingredients except crackers in a lightly greased slow cooker. Cover and cook on high setting for about 30 minutes, or until cheese melts; stir occasionally. Continue to cook on high until mixture is smooth and cheese is melted. Add more milk if necessary; turn to low setting and cook for 3 to 4 hours. Serve with crackers for dipping.

Soups are ideal for casual get-togethers. Borrow 3 or 4 slow cookers and fill each with a different soup, stew or chili. Or, better yet, ask friends to bring their favorite soups to share!

Broccoli-Cheese Soup

Makes 6 to 8 servings

8-oz. pkg. pasteurized
    processed cheese spread,
    cubed
2 10-3/4 oz. cans cream of
    celery soup

1 pt. half-and-half
2 10-oz. pkgs. frozen chopped
    broccoli

Place all ingredients in a slow cooker; cover and cook on low setting
for 6 to 8 hours.

The prettiest croutons...cut bread with a small cookie cutter.
Brush cut-outs with butter, place on a baking sheet and bake
at 350 degrees until golden.

Comforting Potato Soup

Makes 4 to 6 servings

4 to 5 potatoes, peeled and
    cubed
10-3/4 oz. can cream of celery
    soup
10-3/4 oz. can cream of chicken
    soup
1-1/4 c. water

1-1/4 c. milk
7.6-oz. pkg. instant mashed
    potato flakes
Garnish: bacon bits, sour cream,
    green onions, shredded
    Cheddar cheese

Place potatoes, soups and water in a slow cooker. Cover and cook on
high setting until potatoes are tender, about 2 to 3 hours. Add milk
and enough instant mashed potatoes to reach desired consistency,
stirring constantly. Cover and cook 2 to 3 hours longer. Garnish
individual servings as desired.

The most indispensable ingredient of all good home cooking:
love for those you are cooking for.
-Sophia Loren

Beefy Vegetable Soup

Makes 6 servings

1 lb. ground beef, browned and
  drained
15-1/2 oz. can tomato sauce
15-oz. pkg. frozen mixed
  vegetables

14-1/2 oz. can stewed tomatoes
10-1/2 oz. can beef broth
1-1/4 c. water
1-1/2 oz. pkg. onion soup mix

Mix all ingredients together in a slow cooker. Cover and cook on low
setting for 8 to 12 hours.

Invite your friends to a soup supper potluck in cool weather.
Line up slow cookers filled with hearty soups, plus one for
hot cider and one for a fruit cobbler. A basket of breads
completes the menu.

Hearty Ham & Bean Soup

Makes 6 servings

3 c. parsnips, peeled and diced
2 c. carrots, peeled and diced
1 c. onion, chopped
1-1/2 c. dried Great Northern
    beans
5 c. water

1-1/2 lbs. smoked ham hocks
2 cloves garlic, minced
2 t. salt
1/2 t. pepper
1/4 t. hot pepper sauce

Place parsnips, carrots and onion in a slow cooker; top with beans. Add remaining ingredients. Cook on high setting for 6 to 7 hours, or until beans are tender. Remove ham hocks; cut meat into bite-size pieces and discard bones. Return meat to slow cooker; heat through.

Wow them at the next chili cook-off! Serve your favorite chili recipe with a variety of yummy toppings...sour cream, shredded cheese, olives, hot peppers and corn chips.

Grandma's Chili

Makes 4 servings

4 slices bacon, crisply cooked
   and crumbled
1-1/2 lbs. ground beef, browned
   and drained
1 onion, chopped
3 tomatoes, chopped
1/2 c. green pepper, chopped

16-oz. can tomato sauce
2 16-oz. cans kidney beans,
   drained and rinsed
1 clove garlic, minced
1 T. chili powder
2 t. sugar
1 t. salt

Add ingredients to a slow cooker; heat on low setting for 6 to 8 hours.

Here's a neat trick to remove grease from the top of your soup...simply drop in a lettuce leaf. Remove and discard once the grease has been absorbed.

Spicy Taco Soup

Makes 4 to 6 servings

1 lb. ground beef, browned and
    drained
15-oz. can kidney beans,
    drained and rinsed

15-oz. can stewed tomatoes
1-1/4 oz. pkg. taco seasoning
    mix
8-oz. can tomato sauce

Stir ingredients together in a slow cooker. Heat on low setting for 6 to
8 hours, stirring occasionally.

Use a slow cooker for dishes that you would normally cook on the stove. Try stews, chili or even chicken and noodles. It cooks by itself so you have more time with family & friends.

Pioneer Beef Stew

Makes 6 to 8 servings

2 lbs. stew beef, cubed
5 potatoes, cubed
4 carrots, peeled and diced
14-1/2 oz. can diced tomatoes
7-3/4 oz. can pearl onions,
    drained

3 T. instant tapioca, uncooked
1 T. sugar
1 c. water
3/4 T. salt
pepper to taste

Combine all ingredients in a slow cooker. Cook on high setting for 4 to 5 hours.

Only using half an onion? Rub the cut side with butter
or olive oil, store in the fridge in a plastic zipping bag
and it will stay fresh for weeks.

Chow-Down Corn Chowder

Makes 4 servings

6 slices bacon, diced
1/2 c. onion, chopped
2 c. potatoes, peeled and diced
2 10-oz. pkgs. frozen corn
16-oz. can cream-style corn

1 c. water
1-1/4 T. sugar
1-1/2 t. Worcestershire sauce
1-1/4 t. seasoned salt
1/2 t. pepper

Cook bacon in a skillet until crisp. Remove bacon; reserve drippings.
Add onion and potatoes to drippings; sauté for about 5 minutes. Drain
well. Combine all ingredients including bacon in a slow cooker; stir
well. Cook on low setting for 4 to 7 hours.

Hollow out round loaves of country-style bread to serve your soups and stews in...a hearty meal that your whole family will love.

New England Clam Chowder

Makes 6 servings

1 onion, chopped
1/2 c. butter
2 10-3/4 oz. cans clam chowder
2 10-3/4 oz. cans cream of
   potato soup

6-1/2 oz. can minced clams,
   drained
1 qt. half-and-half

In a small skillet, sauté onion in butter until tender. Combine onion, soups and clams in a slow cooker. Heat on low setting for 4 to 6 hours. Add half-and-half during last 2 hours of cooking time.

Serve up hearty sandwiches outside in warm weather.
An old wooden fruit crate serves as a sturdy tray with plenty
of room for dinner plus a frosty bottle of soda!

Scrumptious BBQ Sandwiches   *Makes 12 servings*

3-lb. beef pot roast
1/4 c. water
1/4 c. milk
2 T. vinegar

3 T. Worcestershire sauce
1 t. chili powder
3 c. barbecue sauce
12 hamburger buns

Place roast in a slow cooker. Add water, milk, vinegar, Worcestershire sauce and chili powder. Cook on low for 8 to 10 hours, until meat is very tender. Remove roast and liquid from slow cooker. Shred meat and return to slow cooker with barbecue sauce; cook for an additional 2 hours. Spoon onto hamburger buns.

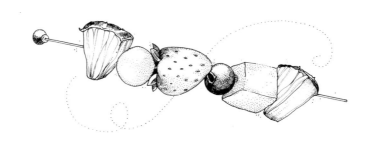

Save time by putting the food processor to work chopping
and dicing veggies...so easy!

Tropical Ham Sandwiches

Makes 12 servings

1-1/2 lbs. cooked ham, finely
    chopped
1 c. brown sugar, packed
1/2 c. Dijon mustard
1/4 c. green pepper, diced
1 T. dried, minced onion
20-oz. can crushed pineapple
12 sandwich buns

Mix all ingredients except buns in a slow cooker. Cover and cook on low setting for 3 to 4 hours. Uncover and cook on high setting for 15 to 30 minutes, until sauce is thickened. Stir and serve on buns.

A slow cooker uses about as much electricity as a light bulb,
making it more economical than using the stove!

Savory French Dip Sandwiches   *Makes 8 servings*

5-lb. boneless beef rump roast
2   10-1/2 oz. cans beef broth
1 onion, finely chopped
1 T. garlic powder
2 t. beef bouillon granules

1/2 t. seasoned salt
1/2 t. dried oregano
1/2 t. dried rosemary
1/4 t. cayenne pepper
8 crusty rolls

Place all ingredients except rolls in a slow cooker. Cover and cook on low setting for 8 to 10 hours or high setting for 4 to 6 hours. Thinly slice meat, reserving broth for dipping. Arrange sliced meat on rolls.

Slow cookers are great for cooking meals while you're out
tag sale-ing...come home to a meal ready to enjoy!

Italian Pork Sandwiches

Makes 8 servings

2 lbs. ground pork, browned
   and drained
15-oz. can pizza sauce
8-oz. can tomato sauce
2 T. vinegar
1 T. Worcestershire sauce
1-1/2 cloves garlic, chopped

1 t. salt
1/2 t. fennel seed
hot pepper sauce to taste
sandwich buns
Garnish: shredded mozzarella
   cheese

Place pork in a slow cooker; stir in sauces and seasonings. Cover and cook on low setting for 8 to 10 hours. Spoon onto buns; top with shredded cheese.

Set out stacks of colorful bandannas...they make super-size
fun napkins when enjoying Sloppy Joes!

Sloppy Joes

Makes 14 to 18 servings

3 c. celery, chopped
1 c. onion, chopped
1 c. catsup
1 c. barbecue sauce
1 c. water
2 T. vinegar
2 T. Worcestershire sauce
2 T. brown sugar, packed

1 t. chili powder
1 t. salt
1 t. pepper
1/2 t. garlic powder
3 to 4-lb. boneless beef chuck
   roast
14 to 18 hamburger buns

Combine all ingredients except roast and buns in a slow cooker; mix well. Add roast; cover and cook on high setting for 6 to 7 hours, until tender. Remove roast; shred meat, return to slow cooker and heat through. Serve on hamburger buns.

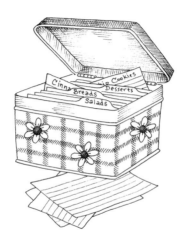

There are so many great-tasting cream soups...mushroom,
celery, onion and chicken. Shake up an old favorite recipe
by trying a different one each time!

Chicken & Green Bean Bake

Makes 4 servings

2 to 3 boneless, skinless
   chicken breasts
salt, pepper and garlic powder
   to taste
10-3/4 oz. can cream of
   mushroom soup

1/2 c. milk
14-1/2 oz. can green beans,
   drained
2.8-oz. can French fried onions

Place chicken in a slow cooker; season with salt, pepper and garlic powder. Cover and cook on high setting for 2 to 3 hours, until juices run clear when chicken is pierced with a fork. Drain. Add soup, milk and green beans; sprinkle onions over top. Cover and cook an additional 30 minutes.

Family always on the go? When everyone can't sit down together for dinner, the slow cooker can provide warm meals for all. With the low, slow heating it's unlikely foods will overcook, so you can keep the main dish warm all evening until everyone gets their share!

Company Apricot Chicken

Makes 4 to 6 servings

1 to 2 lbs. boneless, skinless
    chicken breasts
8-oz. bottle Russian salad
    dressing

12-oz. jar apricot preserves
2 to 3 c. prepared rice

Arrange chicken in a slow cooker; set aside. Combine salad dressing
and preserves; pour over chicken. Cover and cook on low setting for
6 to 8 hours. Serve over a bed of prepared rice.

Be sure to unplug and cool the slow cooker completely
before adding water for cleaning...otherwise, the crockery
or stoneware liner could crack.

Yummy BBQ Chicken

Makes 4 servings

4 boneless, skinless chicken
    breasts
3/4 c. chicken broth

1 c. barbecue sauce
1 sweet onion, sliced
salt and pepper to taste

Place ingredients in a slow cooker; stir gently. Cover and cook on high setting for 3 hours or on low setting for 6 to 7 hours.

Table tents are so handy! Fold a piece of paper in half
and jot down or rubber stamp the recipe name on one side.
Set the table tent next to the slow cooker so everyone will
know just what's for dinner!

Cheesy Chicken

Makes 2 to 4 servings

1-1/2 lbs. boneless, skinless
    chicken breasts
salt, pepper and garlic powder
    to taste
2 10-3/4 oz. cans cream of
    chicken soup

10-3/4 oz. can Cheddar cheese
    soup
3 c. prepared rice, buttered
    noodles or mashed potatoes

Place chicken in a slow cooker; sprinkle with salt, pepper and garlic powder. Pour soups over the top. Cover and cook on high setting for 4 to 6 hours, until chicken falls apart. Spoon over prepared rice, noodles or mashed potatoes.

Slow cookers are ideal for toting to family reunions...they cook away while everyone spends time catching up!

Zesty Picante Chicken

Makes 4 servings

4 boneless, skinless chicken
    breasts
16-oz. jar picante sauce
15-1/2 oz. can black beans,
    drained and rinsed

4 slices American cheese
2 c. prepared rice

Place chicken in a greased slow cooker. Add sauce; spread beans over the top. Cover and cook on low setting for 6 to 8 hours or until juices run clear when chicken is pierced. Top with cheese slices; cover and heat until melted. Spoon over prepared rice to serve.

Make brown & serve dinner rolls extra yummy! Before baking, brush with a little beaten egg and sprinkle with grated Parmesan cheese and Italian seasoning.

That's Amore Chicken Cacciatore *Makes 6 servings*

6 boneless, skinless chicken breasts	2 green peppers, chopped
28-oz. jar spaghetti sauce	1 onion, minced
	2 T. garlic, minced

Place chicken in a slow cooker; top with remaining ingredients. Cover and cook on low setting for 7 to 9 hours.

Chicken with twice the flavor! Let it cool in its broth before
cutting or shredding for slow-cooker recipes.

Chicken-Artichoke Pasta

Makes 4 servings

16-oz. pkg. frozen grilled
    chicken breast strips
1 T. chicken bouillon granules
1/4 c. water
17-oz. jar Alfredo sauce

6-1/2 oz. jar marinated
    artichoke hearts, drained
6-oz. pkg. angel hair pasta,
    cooked

Place chicken strips in a slow cooker with bouillon and water. Cook
on low setting for 2 to 3 hours. Stir in sauce and artichokes; turn slow
cooker to high setting and heat an additional 30 minutes. Serve over
prepared pasta.

A great cooking club theme...slow-cooker recipes only!
Perfect for friends who want to try new recipes and share
delicious food, but don't have all day to prepare.

Chicken Cordon Bleu

Makes 8 to 10 servings

2 eggs
2 c. milk, divided
1 T. dried, minced onion
8 slices bread, cubed and crusts
    removed
12 thin slices cooked ham,
    rolled up

8-oz. pkg. shredded Swiss
    cheese
2-1/2 c. cooked chicken, cubed
10-3/4 oz. can cream of
    chicken soup

Beat eggs and 1-1/2 cups milk together; stir in onion and bread cubes.
Place half of mixture in a slow cooker; top with half of the ham rolls,
cheese and chicken. Combine soup and remaining milk; pour half over
chicken. Repeat layers again, topping with remaining soup mixture.
Cover and cook on low setting for 4 to 5 hours.

Pop Holiday Turkey & Dressing into the slow cooker...then
take it easy and enjoy visiting with your guests!

Holiday Turkey & Dressing

Makes 4 to 6 servings

8-oz. pkg. herb-flavored
    stuffing mix
1/2 c. hot water
2 T. butter, melted
1 onion, chopped
1/2 c. celery, chopped

1/4 c. sweetened, dried
    cranberries
3-lb. boneless turkey breast
1/4 t. dried basil
1/2 t. salt
1/2 t. pepper

Combine stuffing mix, water, butter, onion, celery and cranberries in
a slow cooker; mix well. Sprinkle turkey breast with basil, salt and
pepper; place on top of stuffing mixture. Cover and cook on low
setting for 6 to 7 hours. Remove turkey, slice and set aside. Gently
stir stuffing mixture; let stand for 5 minutes. Spoon stuffing onto a
platter; top with sliced turkey.

Start a tradition...slow-cooker Sunday! Every Sunday
(or whatever day you pick) choose a meal to make in the
slow cooker. Just toss all the ingredients into the slow cooker
and enjoy the day with your family. They will hardly be
able to wait for dinnertime to roll around!

Mom's Spaghetti Sauce

Makes about 5 cups

1 onion, diced
3 cloves garlic, chopped
1 T. butter
3 14-1/2 oz. cans diced
    tomatoes
3 6-oz. cans tomato paste
2 c. water
3 T. olive oil
1 T. dried parsley
1/4 t. salt

1/2 t. pepper
1/2 t. dried basil
1/2 t. dried oregano
1/2 t. garlic powder
1/2 t. dried thyme
2 bay leaves
1/8 t. sugar
16 to 32-oz. pkg. spaghetti,
    cooked

Sauté onion and garlic in butter; set aside. Blend tomatoes and tomato paste in a blender until smooth; pour into a slow cooker. Stir in onion mixture and remaining ingredients except spaghetti. Cover and cook on low setting for about 3 hours, stirring occasionally. Discard bay leaves. Serve over prepared spaghetti.

What a time saver! With a large-capacity slow cooker, you can cook only once for dinner and have enough left over to freeze for another meal. Just divide leftovers into small portions (in freezer-safe containers) and cool quickly in the refrigerator before freezing.

Sauerkraut & Pork

Makes 4 to 6 servings

20-oz. can sauerkraut
1/3 c. brown sugar, packed
1-1/2 lbs. pork sausage links,
    sliced

1 onion, sliced

Combine sauerkraut and brown sugar in a slow cooker; mix well.
Arrange sausage and onion on top. Cover and cook on high setting for
2 hours, adding water if necessary. Reduce heat to low setting; cover
and cook for an additional 2 hours.

As your dish nears the end of its cooking time, check on
the amount of liquid in the slow cooker...if there seems
to be too much, remove the lid and heat on high,
allowing some water to cook out.

Melt-in-Your-Mouth Sausages

Makes 8 servings

8 Italian sausage links
48-oz. can spaghetti sauce
6-oz. can tomato paste
1 green pepper, chopped
1 onion, thinly sliced
1 T. grated Parmesan cheese

1 t. dried parsley
1 c. water
16-oz. pkg. spaghetti, cooked
Garnish: grated Parmesan
   cheese

Place sausages in a skillet; cover with water. Simmer for 10 minutes; drain and slice. Combine all remaining ingredients except spaghetti in a slow cooker; add sausage slices. Cover and cook on low setting for 4 hours. Increase heat to high setting; cook for one additional hour. Serve over prepared spaghetti; sprinkle with Parmesan cheese.

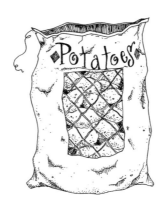

A quick & easy side dish! Roll balls of leftover mashed
potatoes in a mixture of Parmesan cheese and seasoned
bread crumbs...broil until golden brown.

Root Beer Ham

Makes 10 to 12 servings

5-lb. cooked ham   2-ltr. bottle root beer

Place ham in a slow cooker; pour root beer over ham until covered.
Cover and cook on low setting for 3 to 4 hours. Slice and serve.

For best results, always thaw meat before placing it
in a slow cooker.

Country-Style BBQ Spareribs

Makes 4 servings

2 lbs. pork spareribs, cut into
   serving-size pieces
1 T. oil

2 onions, sliced
1-1/2 c. barbecue sauce

In a large skillet, brown ribs in oil over medium-high heat. Reserve drippings; transfer ribs to a slow cooker. Sauté onions in drippings until tender; place in slow cooker. Cover ribs and onions with barbecue sauce. Cover and cook on low setting for 6 to 8 hours, adding a little water if necessary.

Surprisingly, vegetables like potatoes and carrots take longer to cook than meat. Layer veggies on the bottom, then arrange meat on top for the best results.

Scalloped Ham & Potatoes

Makes 4 to 6 servings

4 potatoes, peeled and sliced
2 onions, chopped
1-1/2 c. cooked ham, cubed
2 T. butter
2 T. all-purpose flour

1/2 t. pepper
10-3/4 oz. can Cheddar cheese
  soup
1-1/3 c. water

Layer potatoes, onions and ham in a slow cooker; set aside. Melt
butter in a saucepan over medium heat; stir in flour and pepper until
smooth. Combine soup and water; gradually add to flour mixture.
Bring to a boil; heat and stir until thickened and bubbly. Pour over
ham; cover and cook on low setting for 8 to 9 hours.

Here's a quick tip to make it easy to slice meat into strips or cubes...simply place it in the freezer until barely frozen.

Creamy Beef Stroganoff

Makes 4 to 6 servings

1-1/2 lbs. stew beef, cubed
1 onion, sliced
2 10-3/4 oz. cans cream of
    mushroom soup
2 T. catsup

2 t. Worcestershire sauce
1 t. pepper
1 to 2 c. sour cream
12-oz. pkg. medium egg
    noodles, cooked

Place beef and onion in a slow cooker; set aside. Combine soup, catsup, Worcestershire sauce and pepper; stir into beef mixture. Cover and cook on low setting for 8 to 10 hours. Stir in sour cream and heat through. Spoon over prepared noodles to serve.

Whip up some Parmesan bread! Split an Italian loaf in half and spread with a mixture of 1/4 cup butter, 2 tablespoons grated Parmesan cheese, 2 teaspoons minced garlic and 1/4 teaspoon oregano. Broil until golden...yummy!

Easy Lasagna

Makes 8 servings

1 lb. ground beef
1/2 c. onion, chopped
1 t. garlic, minced
16-oz. can tomato sauce
6-oz. can tomato paste
1 c. water
4-oz. can sliced mushrooms,
    drained

1 t. salt
1 t. dried oregano
8-oz. pkg. lasagna, uncooked
2 c. shredded mozzarella cheese
12-oz. container cottage cheese
1/2 c. grated Parmesan cheese

Brown beef with onion and garlic; drain and spoon into a large bowl.
Add tomato sauce, tomato paste, water, mushrooms, salt and oregano,
mixing well. Spread one-quarter of the meat sauce in the bottom of a
slow cooker; arrange one-third of the uncooked lasagna over the
sauce, breaking if necessary. Combine cheeses; spoon one-third over
lasagna layer. Repeat layers twice; top with remaining meat sauce.
Cover and cook on low setting until lasagna is tender, 4 to 5 hours.

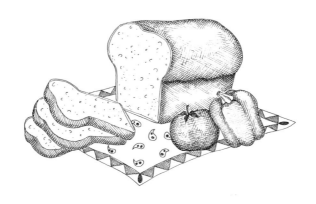

It's so easy to make your own bread crumbs. Dry slices of fresh bread in a 250-degree oven, then tear into sections and pulse in your food processor or blender.

Tried & True Meatloaf

Makes 4 to 6 servings

1-1/2 lbs. ground beef
2 eggs
3/4 c. milk
3/4 c. bread crumbs
1 onion, chopped
1 t. salt

1/4 t. pepper
1/4 c. catsup
2 T. brown sugar, packed
1 t. dry mustard
1/4 t. nutmeg

Combine beef, eggs, milk, bread crumbs, onion, salt and pepper;
mix well. Form into a loaf; place in a slow cooker. Cover and cook on
low setting for 5 to 6 hours. Whisk remaining ingredients together;
pour over meatloaf. Cover and cook on high setting an additional
15 minutes.

Inexpensive, less-tender cuts of beef like chuck roast are perfect for your slow cooker...they'll be fork-tender and delicious after cooking all day.

Pot Roast & Veggies

Makes 4 to 6 servings

2 to 4-lb. beef pot roast
salt and pepper to taste
4 t. all-purpose flour
1/4 c. cold water
1 t. browning sauce

5 potatoes, peeled and cubed
3 carrots, peeled and cubed
2 onions, coarsely chopped
1 clove garlic, minced

Place roast in a slow cooker; sprinkle with salt and pepper. Make a paste of flour and water; stir in browning sauce and spread over roast. Add potatoes, carrots, onions and garlic. Cover and cook on low setting for 8 to 10 hours.

On a cold winter day, it's wonderful to come home to the savory aroma of a home-cooked meal. Don't put your slow cooker away in the summer, though...you can prepare delicious dinners without heating up the house!

Beefy Pot Pie

Makes 4 servings

2-lb. beef round steak, cubed
2 c. plus 3 T. all-purpose flour,
    divided
2 t. salt, divided
1/8 t. pepper
3 potatoes, peeled and sliced
2 carrots, peeled and sliced

1 onion, thinly sliced
16-oz. can whole tomatoes,
    drained
1 T. baking powder
1/4 c. shortening
3/4 c. milk

Place steak cubes in a slow cooker. Combine 3 tablespoons flour, one teaspoon salt and pepper; coat steak thoroughly. Add vegetables; mix well. Cover and cook on low setting for 7 to 10 hours, until tender. Remove steak and vegetables from slow cooker; place in a shallow 2-1/2 quart baking dish. Combine remaining flour, salt and baking powder. Cut in shortening until mixture resembles coarse cornmeal. Add milk; stir well. Pat out on a floured surface; roll out to cover baking dish. Bake, covered, at 425 degrees for 20 to 25 minutes.

Don't forget slow cookers make great traveling companions
for campers and RV'ers. Enjoy all the fun of the great
outdoors, then come in for a delicious dinner.

Swiss Steak

Makes 4 to 6 servings

1-1/2 lbs. beef round steak, cut
    into serving-size pieces
2 T. all-purpose flour
1 t. salt
1/4 t. pepper

1 c. celery, chopped
1 carrot, peeled and chopped
1 onion, sliced
15-oz. can tomato sauce

Place steak in a slow cooker; set aside. Combine flour, salt and pepper;
sprinkle over meat. Mix well. Add vegetables; pour tomato sauce over
all. Cover and cook on low setting for 8 to 10 hours.

Cooking rice for dinner? Make some extra and freeze
one-cup servings in plastic zipping bags. Add veggies
and warm in the microwave for a quick lunch!

Pepper Steak

Makes 6 to 8 servings

1-1/2 to 2 lbs. beef round steak,
   cut into strips
2 t. oil
1/4 c. soy sauce
1 c. onion, chopped
1 clove garlic, minced
1 t. sugar
1/2 t. salt
1/4 t. pepper
1/4 t. ground ginger
14-1/2 oz. can diced tomatoes
2 green peppers, sliced
1/2 c. cold water
1 T. cornstarch
3 to 4 c. prepared rice

Brown beef strips in oil in a skillet. Drain and transfer to a slow cooker;
set aside. Combine soy sauce, onion, garlic and seasonings; pour over
beef strips. Cover and cook on low setting for 5 to 6 hours, until tender.
Add tomatoes and peppers; cover and heat for one additional hour.
Whisk water and cornstarch together; stir into slow cooker. Increase
heat to high setting; heat until thickened, about 15 to 30 minutes.
Serve over prepared rice.

Have frozen leftovers from a previous slow-cooked dinner? Be sure to reheat with the microwave or the conventional oven...the slow-cooking process is not safe for reheating frozen foods.

Saucy Beef & Vegetables

Makes 6 to 8 servings

2 to 3 lbs. beef round steak,
   coarsely chopped
1 onion, chopped
1 green pepper, sliced
2 c. carrots, peeled and chopped
1 zucchini, thinly sliced
1-1/2 oz. pkg. spaghetti sauce
   mix
15-oz. can diced tomatoes
8-oz. can tomato sauce

Place meat in a slow cooker. Add remaining ingredients in order listed.
Cover and cook on low setting for 8 hours.

Pasta or rice may become very soft if cooked all day in a slow cooker. It's best to cook them separately and stir in during the last 20 to 30 minutes, or simply combine with your completed slow-cooker dish as in the Pizza-Rotini Toss.

Pizza-Rotini Toss

Makes 6 to 8 servings

1-1/2 lbs. ground beef
1 onion, chopped
2 10-oz. jars pizza sauce
9.9-oz. jar sliced mushrooms,
    drained

4 c. shredded mozzarella cheese
10-oz. pkg. sliced pepperoni
8-oz. pkg. rotini pasta, cooked

Brown ground beef and onion together in a skillet; drain. Add pizza sauce and mushrooms; heat thoroughly. Layer ground beef mixture, cheese and pepperoni in a slow cooker. Cover and cook on low setting for 8 hours. Toss with prepared rotini before serving.

If you live at high altitude, allow an additional 30 minutes of cooking time for each hour of cooking time that the recipe specifies.

Macaroni & Cheese

Makes 4 to 6 servings

2 c. prepared elbow macaroni
2 T. oil
12-oz. can evaporated milk
1-1/2 c. milk

3 c. pasteurized processed
    cheese spread, shredded
1/4 c. butter, melted
2 T. dried, minced onion

Combine macaroni and oil; toss to coat. Pour into a slow cooker; stir in remaining ingredients. Cover and cook on low setting for 3 to 4 hours, stirring occasionally.

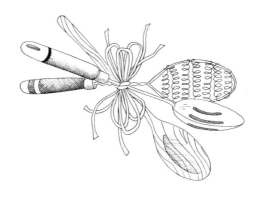

Slow cooking keeps the moisture inside, causing condensation to form on the lid. To avoid spilling into the food, always lift the lid straight up, rather than tilting, when stirring or adding ingredients.

Farmhouse Dressing

Makes 12 to 14 servings

1 c. margarine
1-1/2 c. onion, chopped
2 c. celery, chopped
2 8-oz. cans sliced mushrooms,
   drained
1/4 c. fresh parsley, minced
12 to 13 c. dry bread cubes

1 t. poultry seasoning
1-1/2 t. salt
1 t. dried sage
1 t. pepper
1/2 t. dried marjoram
3 to 4 c. chicken broth
2 eggs, beaten

Melt margarine in a skillet; sauté onion, celery, mushrooms and parsley. Set aside. Place bread cubes in a large bowl; pour mixture over top. Add seasonings and toss together. Pour in enough broth to moisten. Add eggs and mix well. Lightly pack mixture into a slow cooker. Cover and cook on high setting for 45 minutes; reduce to low setting and cook for 4 to 8 hours.

A slow cooker makes a delightful (and welcome)
housewarming or bridal shower gift...be sure to
tie on a few favorite recipes before giving.

Calico Baked Beans

Makes 8 to 10 servings

1 lb. bacon, crisply cooked and
    crumbled
2/3 c. barbecue sauce
1/3 c. catsup
3/4 c. brown sugar, packed
1 t. dry mustard

2 t. cider vinegar
16-oz. can pork & beans
16-oz. can butter beans,
    drained and rinsed
15-oz. can kidney beans,
    drained and rinsed

Mix all ingredients in a slow cooker. Cover and cook on low setting for
2 to 3 hours.

Slow down and enjoy life.
-Eddie Cantor

Fresh Green Beans

Makes 2 to 4 servings

2 lbs. green beans, chopped
1/4 lb. cooked ham, cubed

3 to 4 c. water
1 t. salt

Combine all ingredients in a slow cooker. Cover and cook on low setting for 10 to 12 hours, stirring occasionally.

Roasted Vegetable Pot

Makes 6 to 8 servings

3 c. potatoes, peeled and sliced
3 c. carrots, peeled and sliced

1/2 c. onion, chopped
15-oz. can beef broth

Arrange vegetables in a slow cooker; pour broth evenly over all. Cover and cook on high setting for 4 to 6 hours; mix well before serving.

Place just a corner of a bread slice between your teeth
while you're cutting onions and your eyes won't water.

Loaded Baked Potatoes

Makes 8 to 10 servings

5 lbs. potatoes, peeled, cubed
   and boiled
1/2 c. butter, melted
4 c. shredded sharp Cheddar
   cheese

2 c. sour cream
3-1/4 oz. jar bacon bits
salt and pepper to taste

Combine potatoes and butter in a large bowl. Add cheese, sour cream
and bacon bits, mixing thoroughly. Add salt and pepper to taste.
Spoon mixture into a slow cooker; cover and cook on high setting for
one hour or on low setting for 2 hours, stirring every 30 minutes.

Turn Easy Cheesy Potatoes & Sausage into a hearty
overnight breakfast dish...substitute ham or
precooked breakfast sausage for the Kielbasa.
Mmm...great to wake up to!

Easy Cheesy Potatoes & Sausage   *Makes 4 servings*

32-oz. pkg. frozen hashbrowns,
   partially thawed
1 lb. Kielbasa, chopped

1 onion, diced
10-3/4 oz. can cheese soup
1-1/4 c. milk

Combine all ingredients in a slow cooker; mix well. Cover and cook on high setting for 3 hours or on low setting for 8 to 10 hours.

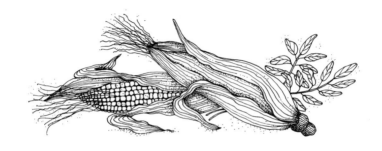

Make herb butter for corn on the cob by mixing butter in a food processor with fresh chopped chives, dill or thyme.

Creamy Corn

Makes 8 servings

2 10-oz. pkgs. frozen corn
2 T. sugar
8-oz. pkg. cream cheese, cubed

1/4 c. butter, diced
6 T. water

Place all ingredients in a slow cooker. Cover and cook on low setting for 4 hours, stirring occasionally.

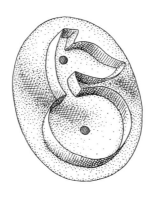

Take along a dessert in a slow cooker to a party or meeting...simply wrap it in a towel to keep it warm. Serve within an hour or plug it in at a low setting.

Country Cherry Cobbler

Makes 6 to 8 servings

2 21-oz. cans cherry pie filling
18-1/2 oz. pkg. yellow cake mix
1/4 c. butter, softened

1/2 c. chopped nuts
Garnish: ice cream or whipped
   topping

Spread pie filling in a slow cooker; set aside. Combine dry cake mix and butter with a fork until coarse crumbs form; sprinkle over pie filling. Sprinkle nuts on top. Cover and heat on low setting for 3 hours. Serve warm with ice cream or whipped topping.

Mini slow cookers are terrific for making sauces and
melting chocolate...keep one on hand.

Peanutty Chocolate Candy

Makes about 8 dozen

1 T. oil
3 T. baking cocoa
24-oz. pkg. white melting
    chocolate, chopped
12-oz. pkg. semi-sweet
    chocolate chips

16-oz. jar unsalted dry-roasted
    peanuts
16-oz. jar salted dry-roasted
    peanuts

Combine all ingredients except nuts in a slow cooker. Cover and cook on high setting until chocolate is melted and smooth, about one hour. Turn off slow cooker; add peanuts and stir well. Drop by teaspoonfuls onto wax paper; let cool.

Put out the welcome mat and invite friends over for dessert...keep it simple so everyone's free to visit.

Triple Chocolate Delight

Makes 8 to 10 servings

18-1/2 oz. pkg. chocolate cake
  mix
3.9-oz. pkg. instant chocolate
  pudding mix
2 c. sour cream
1 c. water

1/2 c. oil
4 eggs, beaten
6-oz. pkg. semi-sweet chocolate
  chips
Garnish: vanilla ice cream or
  whipped topping

Mix all ingredients well; pour into a greased slow cooker. Cover and
cook on low setting for 6 to 8 hours. Serve warm, topped with vanilla
ice cream or whipped topping.

Heat lemons in the microwave for 30 seconds before squeezing...you'll get twice the juice!

Lemon-Poppy Seed Cake

Makes 6 to 8 servings

14-oz. pkg. lemon-poppy seed
    bread mix
1 egg, beaten
8-oz. container sour cream

1-1/4 c. water, divided
1/2 c. sugar
1/4 c. lemon juice
1 T. butter

Mix together bread mix, egg, sour cream and 1/2 cup water until well moistened. Spread in a lightly greased slow cooker; set aside. Combine sugar, lemon juice, butter and remaining water in a small saucepan; bring to a boil. Pour boiling mixture into slow cooker; don't stir. Cover and cook on high setting for 2 to 2-1/2 hours. Edges will be slightly browned. Turn off slow cooker; let stand for 30 minutes with the cover ajar. When cool enough to handle, hold a large serving plate over top of slow cooker, then invert.

Bread pudding is a wonderful way to use up leftover bread.
Try French bread, raisin bread or even extra cinnamon
buns or doughnuts for an extra-tasty dessert!

Sweet & Simple Bread Pudding   *Makes 8 servings*

3 c. bread cubes
1/2 c. raisins
3/4 c. brown sugar, packed
3 eggs, beaten
3-1/2 c. milk

2 t. vanilla extract
2 t. cinnamon
1/2 t. salt
Garnish: warm cream

Mix all ingredients together until bread cubes are thoroughly soaked.
Place in a lightly greased slow cooker. Cover and cook on high setting
for 3 to 4 hours, until a knife inserted into the middle comes out clean.
Serve warm or cold, topped with warm cream.

INDEX

INDEX

How Did Gooseberry Patch Get Started?

Gooseberry Patch started in 1984 one day over the backyard fence in Delaware, Ohio. We were next-door neighbors who shared a love of collecting antiques, gardening and country decorating. Though neither of us had any experience (Jo Ann was a first-grade school teacher and Vickie, a flight attendant & legal secretary), we decided to try our hands at the mail-order business. Since we both had young children, this was perfect for us. We could work from our kitchen tables and keep an eye on the kids too! As our children grew, so did our "little" business. We moved into our own building in the country and filled the shelves to the brim with kitchenware, candles, gourmet goodies, enamelware, bowls and our very own line of cookbooks, calendars and organizers! We're so glad you're a part of our **Gooseberry Patch** family!

For a free copy of our **Gooseberry Patch**
catalog, write us, call us or visit us online at:

Gooseberry Patch
600 London Rd.
★ P.O. Box 190 ★
Delaware, OH 43015

1·800·854·6673
www.gooseberrypatch.com